writing guides

ACTIVITIES FOR Poetry

FRANCESCA KAY

PHOTOCOPIABLE PHOTOCOPIABLE PHOTOC

POETRY
FOR AGES
5-7

CONTENTS

INTRODUCTION

The Scholastic *Writing Guides* series provides teachers with ideas and projects that promote a range of writing, bringing insights from educational research into the classroom. Each guide explores a different type of writing and provides example material, background information, photocopiable activities and teaching suggestions. Their aim is to enable teachers to guide the writing process, share planning ideas and develop themes as a context for writing activities.

The materials:
- motivate children with interesting activities
- break complex types of writing into manageable teaching units
- focus on and develop the typical features of particular types of writing
- provide original approaches to teaching.

Each book is divided into sections, beginning with examples of the type of writing being taught. These are followed by ideas for developing writing and projects that will extend over a series of sessions.

SECTION ONE: USING GOOD EXAMPLES

Section One looks at good examples of the genre, with the emphasis on using texts to stimulate and develop writing. Two example texts are shared, and questions that focus the discussion on their significant features are suggested. This is followed by activities that explore what the texts can teach us about writing, enabling teachers to compare the two texts and to go on to model the type of writing presented in the guide.

SECTION TWO: DEVELOPING WRITING

Section Two moves from reading to writing. This section provides activities that prompt and support children in planning and writing. A range of approaches includes planning templates and strategies to stimulate ideas. The activities refine children's ideas about the type of writing being developed and give them focused writing practice in the context of scaffolded tasks. Teacher's notes support each activity by explaining the objective and giving guidance on delivery.

SECTION THREE: WRITING

Section Three moves on to writing projects. Building upon the earlier work in Section Two, these projects aim to develop the quality of writing and provide a selection of ideas for class or group work on a particular theme or idea. The teacher may choose to use some or all of the ideas presented in each project as a way of weaving the strategies developed in Section Two into a more complex and extended writing task.

SECTION FOUR: REVIEW

Section Four supports the assessment process. Children are encouraged to reflect on the type of writing they are tackling and to evaluate how effectively their work has met the criteria for the genre identified in Section One.

Ten green dragons

In the cave dwelt dragons ten.
One fell fighting four horsemen.

In the cave dwelt dragons nine.
One went down the deep, dark mine.

In the cave dwelt dragons eight.
Two forgot to hibernate.

In the cave dwelt dragons six.
One dropped dead from politics.

In the cave dwelt dragons five.
One took a dive in overdrive.

In the cave dwelt dragons four.
One got struck by a meteor.

In the cave dwelt dragons three.
One ran off with a chimpanzee.

In the cave dwelt dragons two.
One went onto the King's menu.

In the cave dwelt dragons one.
Laid ten eggs and then was gone.

Nick Toczek

Catch a little rhyme

Once upon a time
I caught a little rhyme

I set it on the floor
but it ran out the door

I chased it on my bicycle
but it melted to an icicle

I scooped it up in my hat
but it turned into a cat

I caught it by the tail
but it stretched into a whale

I followed it in a boat
but it changed into a goat

When I fed it tin and paper
it became a tall skyscraper

Then it grew into a kite
and flew far out of sight...

Eve Merriam

Poetry provides a link between the spoken and written word, and between the worlds of reality and imagination. Many children of this age are already acquainted with poems through nursery rhymes and action rhymes. They enjoy hearing them, saying them and reading them over and over again. Many of these well-loved verses have led children into the experience of reading and writing. Poems can introduce rhyme and rhythm, repeating patterns, use of description, and writing within frameworks and in different formats. Poems are wonderful for shared and individual reading. They can make an accessible introduction to humour in writing and to the possibilities for exploring the imagination.

The poems on the two photocopiable pages in this section can be used to explore particular aspects of the genre. They both have rhyme, a rhythmic pattern and humour, and show that poetry can take many forms.

Shared activities

Ten green dragons

Use the counting poem on photocopiable page 4 to introduce patterned language and rhyme. These are very important elements in poetry, although they don't always appear together and sometimes not at all. Read the poem to the children, then point out the counting element and discuss the repetition in the verses. The recurring *In the cave dwelt dragons...* builds the poem towards its ending, and also helps understanding of its content.

Show the children how the poem is arranged, in verses of two lines each. Explain that couplets (literally a couple of lines) are a popular poetic form. Ask the children if they can hear and see where the rhymes are, and note that they are arranged in pairs. Stress the importance of the position of the rhymes at the end of the lines. Then look at how the rhyming parts of the words are spelled, emphasising that it is only the *sound* of a rhyme that is important.

Can the children spot the missing number? Discuss why the poet left it out. (Just about the only rhymes for *seven* are *heaven* and *eleven*, which doesn't give a poet much scope!)

Catch a little rhyme

The nonsense poem on photocopiable page 5 uses repetitive language, but more subtly and less consistently than the previous poem. Having read the poem, notice the repetition in the middle verses: *I [verb] it... / but it...*, and the different verbs, which help to give the poem its pace and excitement. It is also written in couplets, each one forming part of the story. Can the children see that the rhymes in this poem are in the same places as 'Ten green dragons'?

Re-read the first couplet and ask the children if they know where the first line has been 'borrowed' from. Perhaps using the opening words from a fairy tale indicates that this will be a strange, magical poem. 'Catch a little rhyme' has a very unreal subject. How could someone catch a rhyme, as it has no body, and how could it change into all those strange things? This is a chance to point out that anything can happen in a poem. Poets can let their imaginations go wild, not limited by the real world.

Read the last couplet, and see if the children think it's really the end. Has the rhyme been caught? Could the poem continue? Discuss how the ellipsis tells us it is not the end of the poem nor the story. If there had been a full stop, it would have given a very different meaning.

Planning a counting poem

Now work on photocopiable page 8 together. Ask the children to think of rhymes for the numbers and then to think of a subject for a counting poem, such as cats or ducklings, cars or bicycles, kings or queens. Referring to 'Ten green dragons' for the placement of rhymes, ask the children to devise one or two couplets, using the information collected on the sheet. Highlight the repeating structure of the first lines of couplets in 'Ten green dragons' and the middle of 'Catch a little rhyme' and help the children to include something similar in their plans.

Chasing little rhymes

The activity on photocopiable page 9 will help the children to notice rhyme and appreciate where rhyming words are placed. Encourage them to remember the lines in 'Catch a little rhyme' that tell what the poet did to the rhyme she caught (not including the first verse). Remind them how each of those lines ends. Then do the same for what happened to the rhyme. Ask the children to write the end words in sequence in the boxes on the sheet, then to look at the pairs of rhymes, one above the other. Advise them to read the rhymes out loud to make sure they work. What do they notice about the spellings of the pairs of rhymes? Do they have to be spelled the same?

Taking ideas further

Draw attention to the sounds of rhymes as you read aloud. You could try a 'rhyme challenge' – making up first lines of couplets in the style of 'Catch a little rhyme', and asking the children to provide the second, rhyming, line. For example: *I threw it into the sky* (rhymes could be *fly, try, cry*); *I sailed it on the sea* (*free, bee, me*); *I sat it on a log* (*dog, frog, jog*). This game will highlight the way rhyme works and show how the second line of a couplet continues the sense of the first.

When looking for subjects for poems, you might take your own classroom as inspiration and ask the children to create rhymes for objects around them, themselves or their friends. You could also help them to write class rules with rhymes: poetry can be as much about wordplay and enjoyment of language as form and content.

Comparing two rhyming poems

Photocopiable page 10 can be used for individual writing or as a shared activity. Talk about common features of the poems on pages 4 and 5, looking at couplets, rhymes and where rhymes can be found. Ask if either poem changes its pattern, and how and why the pattern changes. Encourage the children to think how they could invent or adapt their own ideas for a poem in this format. You could go on to find and compare other poems written in a similar style.

Recipe for a poem

Photocopiable page 11 can be enlarged and used as a prompt sheet as the children begin their writing. Explain that when you follow a recipe, you need to find the right ingredients and mix them carefully to make something good. It's the same with a poem. Relate the 'ingredients' on the sheet to the poems on pages 4 and 5, noting that not all the ingredients are used in each. Through reading and hearing a range of poems, children will gain valuable experience of other ingredients used in poetry. They will begin to recognise patterns and understand the value of rhymes. Look at a few poems and ask the children to work out their ingredients, with reference to page 11. This will build their understanding of verse and give them different examples to think about when writing their own poetry in Sections Two and Three.

Planning a counting poem

Think of one or two rhymes for each of these numbers.

ten

_____

_____

nine

_____

_____

eight

_____

_____

seven

_____

_____

six

_____

_____

five

_____

_____

four

_____

_____

three

_____

_____

two

_____

_____

one

_____

_____

Who or what will the poem be about?

_____

How is each couplet going to start?

_____

Have a go at writing a couplet here.

_____

Chasing little rhymes

What did the poet do to the rhyme? What word comes at the end of each line that tells you?

What happened to the rhyme each time? What word is at the end of each of those lines?

Write the pairs of rhymes together. Do the spellings match?

writing guides: **POETRY**

Comparing two rhyming poems

They look the same, but...

Compare the two poems. Put a tick ✔ by the sentences that are true and a cross X by the false ones.

1. They both have couplets. ☐

2. They put their rhyming words at the end of each line. ☐

3. They are both counting poems. ☐

4. They are both about catching rhymes. ☐

5. Both poems use a repeating pattern in the first line of each couplet. ☐

6. Neither poem has really ended. ☐

How many statements are false? _____

How many are true? _____

Write some more true or false sentences about the poems.

_____

_____

_____

_____

_____

_____

Recipe for a poem

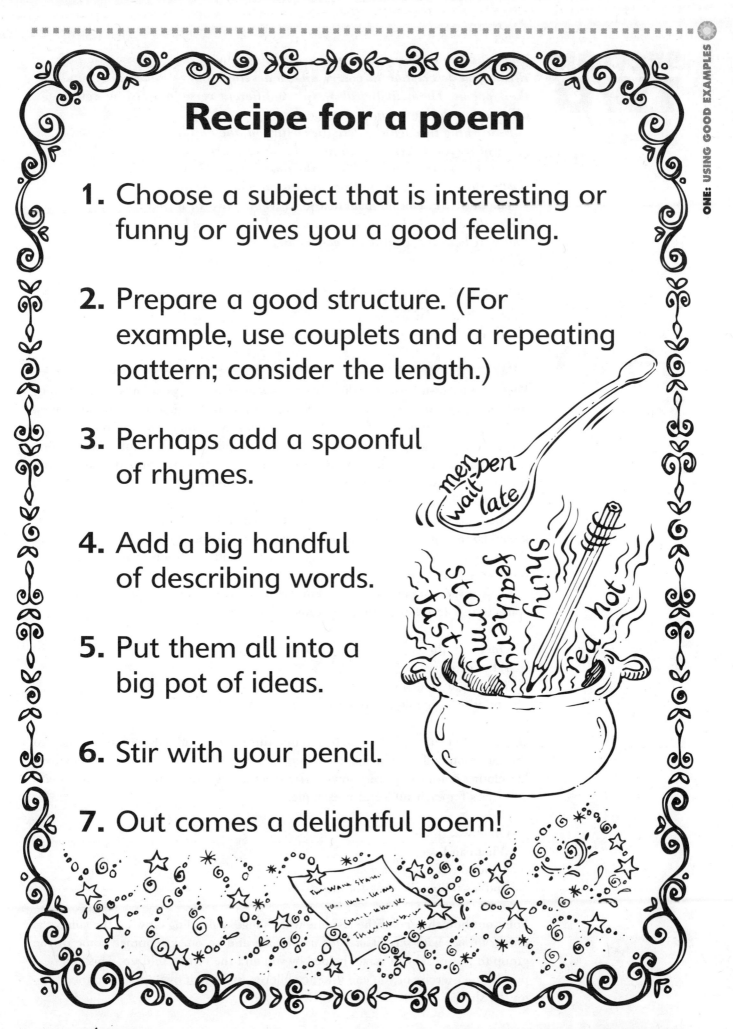

1. Choose a subject that is interesting or funny or gives you a good feeling.

2. Prepare a good structure. (For example, use couplets and a repeating pattern; consider the length.)

3. Perhaps add a spoonful of rhymes.

4. Add a big handful of describing words.

5. Put them all into a big pot of ideas.

6. Stir with your pencil.

7. Out comes a delightful poem!

SECTION TWO
DEVELOPING IDEAS

The activities in this section will help children with their appreciation of rhyme and description in poetry, and in developing their vocabulary to use in their poems. The activities also explore different verse formats, as well as alliteration, humour and nonsense verse.

In working through the activities with you, the children will be building a bank of useful descriptive words and phrases, forms of rhyme and different frames for poetry. They will have the opportunity to explore and engage with poetry through your modelling, discussion and their own written exercises.

The activities can be modelled for a whole class or a smaller group before the children begin independent work. All can be used as shared activities that will help less confident readers and writers.

WHAT'S IT LIKE?
WHAT YOU NEED
Photocopiable page 18, writing materials.

WHAT TO DO
Poets almost always use describing words in some way. They can make poems lively, interesting and moving. Make the children aware of the importance of adjectives, and suggest we should try to use them in poems and stories, and in our everyday speech too. Working as a group on the photocopiable sheet, think of describing words that could be applied to the various pictures. Stress the importance of using the most effective words, which are not always the first ones thought of. For instance, when describing the elephant, ask if there are interesting words to use instead of *big*: perhaps *massive*, *huge*, *giant* or *gigantic*. The rain could be more than just *wet*, it could be *damp*, *dripping*, *drenching* or *splashing*. Encourage the children to extend the search for adjectives by looking in books or in classroom wall displays, and these could be added to the sheet.

Look at the last part of the sheet and read out this example of a short verse that starts to use describing words to fit into a poetic pattern:

> One, two, three,
> What can I see?
> The bright golden sun,
> And it's shining down on me.

Discuss other things that could be put into this pattern: animals perhaps; objects in the classroom; different people; anything in the natural world; aspects of ourselves, like clothes or toys. Improvise some verses together, using at least two of the children's adjectives for each subject, for example:

> One, two, three
> What can I see?
> A round ticking clock,
> And it's telling the time for me.

Point out how the end of the last line will change depending on what the subject is doing: *to me*, *with me*, *at me*, *for me*, *by me* and so on. Encourage some of the group to try speaking a verse, helped by you and the other children. This can be a purely oral exercise or you can ask the children to fit their own verse into the frame on the sheet.

Ask the children to complete the sheet individually or in small groups. Suggest that the sheets will be a very useful reference for all types of writing that they undertake, not just poetry.

I LIKE THE WEATHER

WHAT YOU NEED

Photocopiable page 19, writing materials, board or flip chart.

OBJECTIVES
■ To explore rhymes.
■ To follow a pattern in writing a poem.

WHAT TO DO

Rhymes are an important part of poetry. Not all poems rhyme of course, but young writers should have experience of making rhymes, and understanding how and where to place them in their verses.

Pie Corbett's poem 'I like colours' has a very simple rhyming structure. Read these verses to the children (or the whole poem if you have a copy).

> I like blue.
> I like the sky
> where birds fly high.
>
> I like yellow.
> I like the sun
> when we have fun.

See if the children can identify which words rhyme and notice that they come at the end of the lines.

Use the first verse of the poem, about the colour blue, as a model. Write *I like blue* at the top of the board, explaining this is the first line of the verse. For something blue, write *I like the sky* underneath, and explain to the children that you want to find rhymes for this line. Ask if anyone can think of rhyming words to go with *sky*, for example *fly*, *butterfly*, *pie*, *my*, *eye*, *cry* and *dry*. List the rhyming words on the board, then make a verse for the children, for example:

> I like blue,
> I like the sky
> where I saw a butterfly.
>
> I like blue,
> I like the sky
> as the clouds float by.

Point out that not all words that rhyme are useful all the time. *Pie*, for instance, is probably useless for your verse called 'I like the sky'!

You could add another verse to the 'blue' poem, such as *I like the sea*. Write that line on the board, and ask for rhymes for *sea* (*free*, *me*, *tea*, *bee*, *ski*, *key…*). Using the rhymes, encourage the children to make little verses, for example:

> I like the sea
> splashing up to my knee.
>
> I like the sea
> where the fish swim free.

Watch out for rhymes that don't fit the context, but suggest that they might be useful another time. Make sure that the verses make sense as well as contain rhyme.

I like... makes a simple structure and is an adaptable frame for a poem, whether spoken or written. Try briefly with other subjects, such as different foods, before asking the children to work on the photocopiable sheet. Look at the different types of weather pictured, and discuss possible rhyming words to use. Advise the children to look at the verse examples on the board to help them with composing their rhymes. This can be completed individually or in pairs.

ALLITERATION
WHAT YOU NEED
Paper, writing materials, board or flip chart.

OBJECTIVES

■ To understand alliteration.
■ To make alliterative poetry lines and tongue-twisters.

WHAT TO DO
Alliteration has been an important part of poetry for hundreds of years. It was a key part of Anglo-Saxon poetry for example, and was widely in use long before rhyme. It can make very effective descriptive sentences and short poems. Finding alliterative words really tests a child's vocabulary and ingenuity, but is ultimately very satisfying, both in spoken and written forms.

Explain to the children that alliteration is the repetition of a letter sound at the beginning of words in a sentence or short phrase. Try modelling some simple alliterations, using the first names of the children in the class. Write each name on the board, and then add a suitable alliterative description. Examples could be *Cheerful Charlie, Joking Jack, Happy Hassan* or *Smiling Sarah*. Ask the children to think of other suitably positive describing words. This is also a good way of introducing children new to each other. The effort of remembering the little description helps to fix each name in the mind.

Once you have a list of alliterative names, extend the activity by thinking of a whole phrase to go with some of them. Remember that each phrase does not have to be very long! For example:

Cheerful Charlie chewed some chocolate.
Happy Hassan hopped home in a hurry.
Running Rhiannon raced with a rabbit.

Make sure everyone can hear the alliteration, then encourage the children to make a phrase for their own name, starting with the adjective you have already found for them. Point out that not *every* word in the alliterative phrase has to start with the alliterative letter, as this would make the task difficult, if not impossible. Looking at your examples, talk about which little words – *and, a, of, on, the, was, in*, for example – are useful for making such phrases work.

Little bits of alliteration can sound very effective in most types of poetry, so ask the children to keep it in mind when they are writing other poems. Listen for alliteration in everyday speech, as many instances occur without us thinking about it. You will discover that some letters are very good for this activity, others are more challenging. Try to steer clear of x, z, k,q and v, unless of course one of your children's names starts with one of those letters; in which case, be prepared for a big think!

To continue this activity independently, ask the children to choose five letters to make lists of alliterative words and then use one list to make up a poetic phrase. The lists will prove useful reference when writing other poems, even if those poems aren't specifically alliterative.

writing guides: **POETRY**

OUT AND ABOUT WITH POETIC PETS
WHAT YOU NEED
Photocopiable page 20, writing materials, board or flip chart.

WHAT TO DO
Read out 'On Holiday with Grandma' by Robin Mellor.

OBJECTIVE
- To work on description and the use of verbs in poetry.
- To use a list form for writing a poem.

> When we took Grandma to the beach
> she dug a deep hole in the wet sand,
> knocked down my row of castles,
> caught red crabs in the rock pools,
> went in the sea right up to her knees,
> walked in some clay
> so it squished through her toes,
> tied long, green seaweed in her hair,
> played cricket, had an ice cream,
> and threw a bucket of water over Dad.
> Grandma said she had not had so
> much fun for years.

Point out that the humour comes from Grandma doing lots of things unexpected of an old lady. Some of what she does is also considered to be 'naughty', like knocking over the sandcastles and throwing water over Dad; things we might like to do, but are now too grown-up or well behaved!

Help the children to see that the poem is made up of a list of what Grandma does, and each new item on the list is written on its own line. Use of this form can make for a very effective poem. Emphasise the verbs that help to make the poem so lively, and point out that nearly every line starts with a verb. This structure will be useful when devising group or individual verses.

Re-read the poem, drawing attention to the descriptive phrases: *deep hole, wet sand, red crabs, long green seaweed.* Think about devising a class poem in a similar style, first choosing a relative to be the poem's subject. It works best with someone very old or very young, as they don't always behave as well as we do! Then choose a location to take them. Grandad could go to school or to the funfair; little brother to the library, the swimming pool or sports day; baby sister to play football or to a posh restaurant. Ask the children what their subject might do, and make a list of the verbs that will form the first word of each line of the poem. Write the opening line in the same form as Robin Mellor and devise a poem together. For example:

> When we took little sister to a restaurant,
> she threw a silver spoon at the waiter,
> picked hot roast potatoes with her fingers,
> spilled her sticky soup on the table,
> knocked over a shiny glass of water,
> rubbed gooey tomato sauce into her hair,
> squished her hands into her melting ice cream,
> shouted very loudly I WANT MORE!!
> Little sister said she rather liked
> eating out.

It's a lovely format for reading out loud or adapting for performance, perhaps with everyone together saying the first and last lines.

writing guides: **POETRY**

Discuss other possible subjects for a poem in this style. They don't have to be human and could be fantastical. Perhaps someone could be taking a puppy to school where it would chew the books, bark at the teacher, howl during singing, fall asleep after dinner. How about taking a dragon to a birthday party where it might accidentally tread on the cake, knock everyone over by swishing its tail, scratch the floor with its claws while dancing and set fire to the birthday cards? After sharing a few examples like these, let the children have a go for themselves by working through the photocopiable sheet.

JUST IMAGINE!

WHAT YOU NEED

Photocopiable page 21, writing materials, board or flip chart.

OBJECTIVE

■ To examine nonsense verse and consider how to write it.

WHAT TO DO

Explain to the children that nonsense verse takes us into a world where nothing is the same as in our own world. Read out the following poem and ask the children what is unusual about the content. (*Topsy-turvy* means 'upside down', and to appreciate this poem, the children will need to be thinking of everything in reverse, upside down and inside out.)

> I got up in the night to run to school,
> I went for a walk in the swimming pool,
> The fish flapped their wings and sat in the trees,
> The cars all sailed upon the seas.
>
> A great big boat drove down the lane,
> And I stayed dry in the pouring rain,
> The sun shone at night, the moon by day,
> And none of the children wanted to play!
>
> Up in the sky my garden grew,
> Through the air some snails flew,
> The stars all twinkled on the ground,
> In this topsy-turvy town!

Discuss the upside-down world of this nonsense poem, and brainstorm ideas about how other things would be in that world. Write the children's ideas on the board, and check with them that there is some kind of logic to the statements, even though the ideas are absurd. Some questions to start them thinking could be:
● When would we wake up? (At night or when we were tired.)
● When would we go to school? (At the weekend, in the holidays or during the night.)
● Where would we wear our socks? (On our hands.)
● When would we eat? (When we're completely full.)
● How would the sun make us feel? (Freezing cold.)
Stress to the children that the poems you are going to create now do not have to rhyme, as the strange ideas are the most important element this time. Together, arrange the ideas on the board into more verses for the poem. Suggest that writing in the first person – using *I* and *me* – can make a poem sound immediate and truthful. When you are all happy with the way you have continued the poem, you could use these style points to generate a new poem on a similar vein, for example

writing guides: **POETRY**

'A day in school', 'My birthday party' or 'In the sea'. Make sure that whatever happens in the poem is the opposite of normal!

Ask the children to use some or all of the pictures on the photocopiable sheet as subjects or settings for their own nonsense poem. Ask them first to note down their ideas and plan the poem's structure before they write out any lines or verses. They might want to write just one line about each picture or several lines about it. To finish the activity, ask the children to write *Just imagine* as the first line of their poem, listing their ideas underneath to form draft lines.

Ask the children to look for more nonsense poems in books at home and in school. See if they can identify the patterns and frameworks and use them to make new poems. Almost any children's poem by Spike Milligan will provide a fabulous example of nonsense verse. One of the finest and funniest is the immortal 'In the ning nang nong'.

LOOK AT ME
WHAT YOU NEED
Photocopiable page 22, writing materials.

WHAT TO DO
Explain to the children that for this poem, they are going to describe their facial features: ears, eyes, nose and mouth, and what each of these can do. Using an enlarged copy of the photocopiable sheet, read the example adjectives together and ask the children if they can think of any more that could be added.

Then look at the right-hand side of the sheet and brainstorm different things we can do with the features. For example: ears can hear beautiful music, a friend chatting, cars roaring past or a dog barking; eyes can see a colourful rainbow, a shiny apple, the sunlight shining; your nose can smell a delicious dinner, a sweet rose, the muddy field; your mouth can sing a pretty song, whisper a secret, shout across the playground.

Using the verse frame at the bottom of the sheet, create a spoken example, all about yourself, and ask the children if they think it's a good description! Encourage the children to think of words that suit themselves to add to their own copy of the sheet, along with some fun, unlikely and interesting things that their different features might be able to do. Then ask them to combine these ideas to create their self-portraits in poetry.

The *Look at me…* format can be extended into the world of nature or fiction. Particularly useful are characters from traditional tales with which the children are familiar, such as Snow White, Cinderella or Jack:

Look at me,
My grubby ears can hear Mum saying, 'Have you sold the cow?'
My shiny eyes can watch the beanstalk growing high,
My freckled nose can smell the giant as he comes near,
My open mouth can say, 'I don't want to be the giant's dinner.'

The use of fictional characters can make an effective group poem, with each child taking one feature and devising the description, then putting them together to complete the verse. When including animals, look for chances to extend the children's vocabulary, for example a bird's *beak* or elephant's *trunk*.

writing guides: POETRY

What's it like?

Write some words to describe each picture. Then draw your own object to describe.

Choose one picture and use the words in this poem:

One, two, three

What can I see?

The _____

And its _____ at me.

I like the weather

Write some rhyming words for each type of weather.

sun	**rain**	**snow**
fun	lane	go
wet	**cold**	**sleet**
yet	old	feet

Choose two types of weather to write verses about.
Make sure you put your rhyming words in the right place.

I like _____

_____

I like _____

_____

Out and about with poetic pets

What pet would you like to take out?
Choose one and circle its picture.

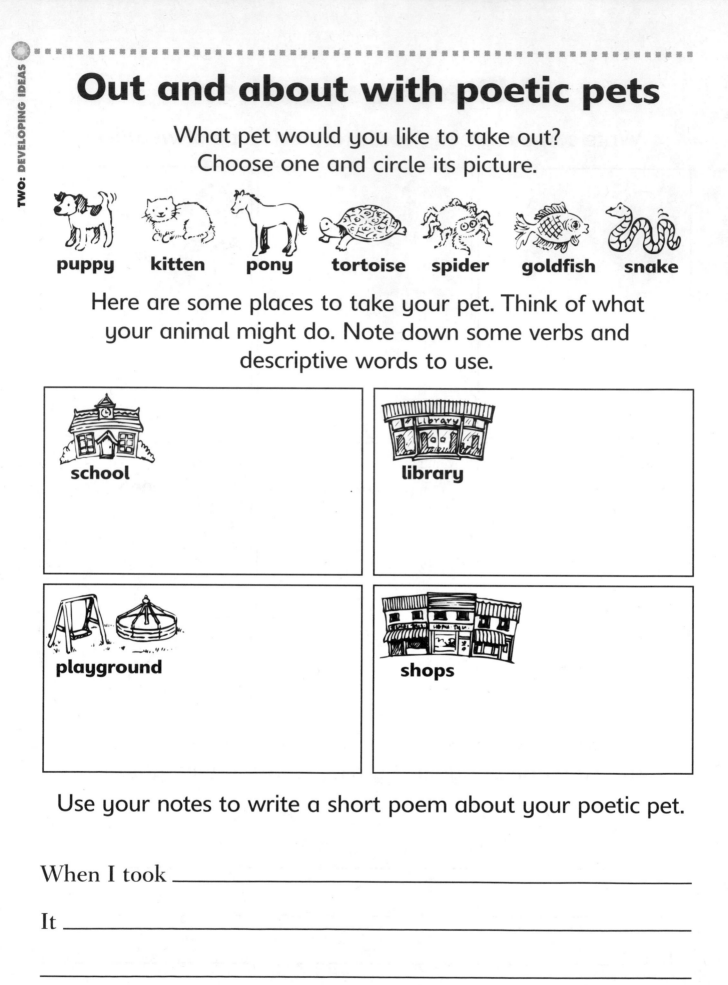

puppy   kitten   pony   tortoise   spider   goldfish   snake

Here are some places to take your pet. Think of what your animal might do. Note down some verbs and descriptive words to use.

school

library

playground

shops

Use your notes to write a short poem about your poetic pet.

When I took _____

It _____

_____

_____

writing guides: POETRY

Just imagine!

Look at the pictures and try to imagine each object in a nonsense world. What would it be like? What would it do? What would happen? Note your ideas beneath the pictures.

Use your ideas to write a short nonsense poem.
Start with **Just imagine...**

Look at me

What are your **ears** like?

neat
listening
wiggling

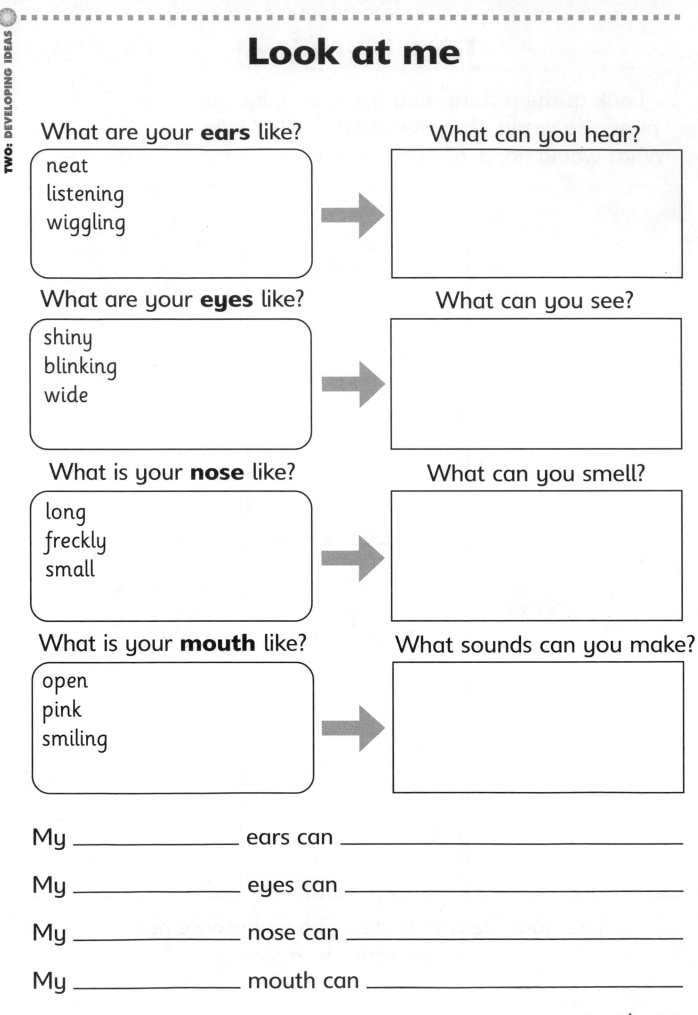

What can you hear?

What are your **eyes** like?

shiny
blinking
wide

What can you see?

What is your **nose** like?

long
freckly
small

What can you smell?

What is your **mouth** like?

open
pink
smiling

What sounds can you make?

My _____ ears can _____

My _____ eyes can _____

My _____ nose can _____

My _____ mouth can _____

By now, the children will have been through activities showing them a number of features of writing poetry. They should have an awareness of:
- *patterns – such as the use of repetition*
- *description – the importance of describing words and lively language*
- *rhymes – exploring, reading, speaking and finding them*
- *alliteration and tongue-twisters*
- *different forms – couplets, lists and so on*
- *nonsense verse – humour, looking at things in a topsy-turvy way.*

After exploring these aspects of poetry, the children should be able to start creating their own poems. The photocopiable pages in this section can prompt the writers and guide them as they begin to write.

How poems look

Before the children get stuck in to writing their own verses, it is worth discussing the look of a poem on the page. Remind the children that poetry looks very different from any other type of writing. The activities so far have carefully guided the children through the potential minefield of the art of writing in lines by giving them easily workable frames. Much of their understanding of form will now be instinctive and guided by their writing experience. Giving a simple writing frame, such as 'Look at me' in Section Two, helps to give young poets a feel for how a poem looks as it is created.

To extend this understanding, compare a poem with a story that has a lot of text on the pages. What differences can the children see? For example, the lengths of the lines, where the full stops and commas are placed, where capital letters are and how the words are arranged on each page. Familiarity with the look of poetry, and how different it is from other types of writing, will help young writers as they create their own verses. Poems are most similar in look to songs; indeed verses of songs often sound like poems when read instead of sung. Were the children to compare printed versions of a rhyming poem and a song, there would be little difference between them.

Poets write in lines, whatever form their poem takes. Help the children to understand that a line is often similar to a short sentence, although it could be no more than a word or couple of words placed together. Each line is written on its own line of the page. They are not written next to each other until the page margin like the continuous text of a story. Make sure the children can see the lines of any poem they study or write, knowing how they are to be arranged on the page, one beneath the other. Explain that this can make the poem sound good and easier to read and understand.

To make a simple frame for a poem, first decide on a topic. Also decide on a certain number of poetic descriptions or phrases that you'd like the children to write, asking them to write the numbers in order down the margin of their sheet of paper. Then ask them to put one phrase or idea next to each number, remembering to stay within the given topic. This challenges the writers to consider how each line should start. Remind them that their lines don't have to be full sentences and could be just a couple of describing words. The numbers can be left out of the final draft, and with the addition of capital letters and punctuation, a basic poetic form appears. You can add to the frame by devising a first and/or last line for everyone to use to enclose their descriptions.

The idea of a poem as a simple list is also found in the ever-popular acrostic verse form, where a word, made up of the first letter of each line, is spelled out down the page. This can be particularly effective as a self-portrait poem, the poet

The seasons

Write a poem on the subject of seasons.
What type of poem would you like to write?

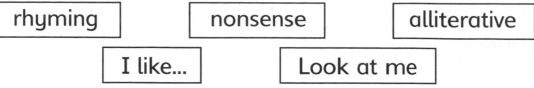

| rhyming | nonsense | alliterative |

| I like... | Look at me |

Think of ways to describe each season. Write some words and phrases to fit the style you have chosen.

spring

summer

autumn

winter

Now write the opening lines or a full first draft of your poem.

The blossom tree of rhyme

Add as many rhymes as you can.

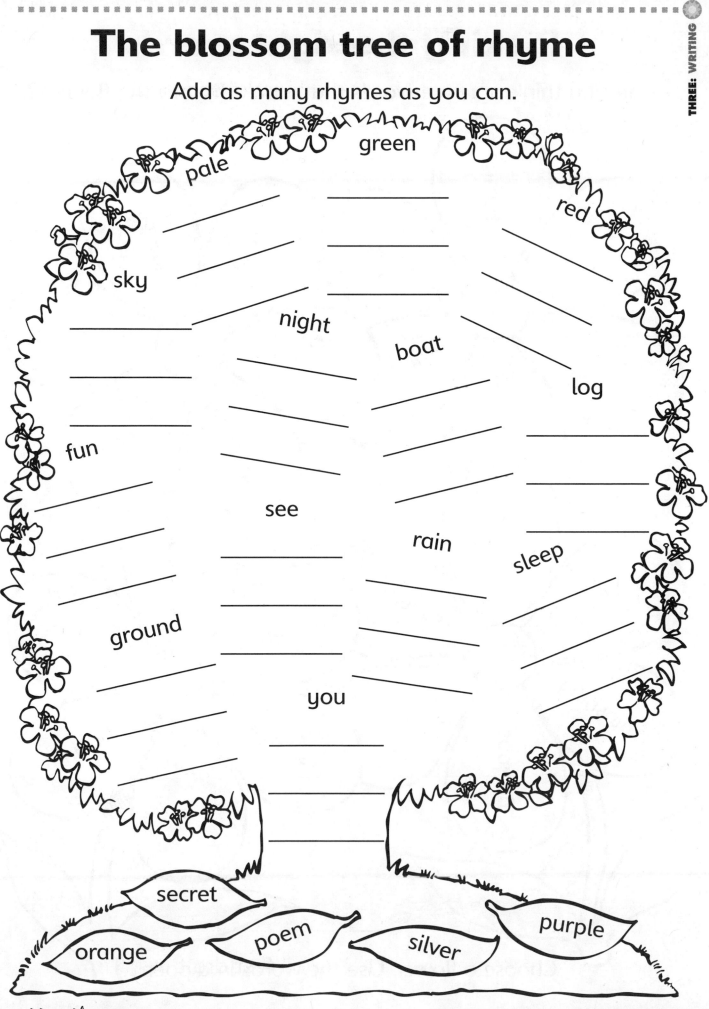

pale

green

red

sky

night

boat

log

fun

see

rain

sleep

ground

you

secret

orange

poem

silver

purple

Picking the right words

Can you think of more words that would fit into the flowers?

titchy
tiny
small
teeny

shiny
sparkly
glittering
bright
scorching

wet
squelchy
splashing
soaking

hot
sizzling
boiling

Choose a flower. Use the words in a poem.

Looking out of the window

Before writing a poem, a poet thinks very hard and gets ready to use attractive words and great ideas.

Try looking out of the window. Remember a poet can see something real...

...or something amazing they have **imagined**.

Different poets see different things.

Why not look out of a window? Write a poem about what **you** can see.

Reviewing the children's poems will help you and them to appreciate how effectively they have used all they have learned; from understanding that poetry can take many forms, but is different from other writing forms, to the world of imagination that a poet can explore. The children's vocabulary development can also be indicated in their poems.

Review the poems while they are being created. Stop to look at the work in progress and see if it has description; if there are rhymes, see how well they work; check the poem is in the right format. Any feedback from this can go straight into the poem, altering and improving it as it is drafted.

Children's self-assessment

Encourage the children to look constantly at their work and ask themselves questions about it: *Does this make sense? Am I sure of the form of the poem I'm writing in? Am I using effective describing words? How are my rhymes coming along? Does the poem have a pattern? Does it sound good when I read it out loud?* Try to instil a desire for improving a poem, for changing it to make it sound and look better.

Sharing a poem with a partner is a positive and useful reviewing method. Hearing a poem will often help with working out what to change and also what sounds really good. Encourage sympathetic and constructive comments. Tell the children to say what they like about someone's poem, perhaps suggest a different idea and discuss with the poet what he or she thinks about the poem. Stress that when commenting on another's work, it is worth remembering always to be positive and encouraging. When poems are finished, there is nothing better than to have a poetry reading, with everyone listening to and enjoying each other's poems.

A poet writes

Photocopiable page 31 provides a framework for children to assess their work. It reminds them of the main features of their poem and helps them to evaluate how easy or difficult it was to compose as well as how successful they think it is.

A reader writes

Photocopiable page 32 is in a similar format to 'A poet writes', but is for a reader or listener to assess someone else's poem, picking out what they liked and explaining why. This review should also generate suggestions for a topic and a form for the writer's next poem. Remind the children to be positive, constructive and civilised!

Teacher assessment

In reviewing the children's work, you might like to think about the following points.
● Was the writer clear about his or her task?
● Description – was it sufficient and clear? Was the child's vocabulary extended?
● Rhyme – has the writer understood and used it correctly?
● Patterned language – has the poet stuck to the pattern or altered it in such a way to show they understood it before changing it?
● Form – has the writer shown they understand alliteration, a list poem, couplets, an *I like…* poem, a self-portrait poem, nonsense verse?

It is important to remember that poetry from this age group isn't meant to be great literature. Don't lower your expectation of each child, but be aware that everyone works to their own limits of vocabulary, experience and aptitude for poetry. Aim to extend those limits and work towards every writer experiencing and enjoying poetry in its many forms.

A poet writes

Title of poem:

My poem was about

I used describing words:

My poem was in this form:

The most difficult part of writing my poem was

The part of my poem I like the best is

A reader writes

Title of poem:

This poem was about

My favourite word (say why) is:

My favourite phrase (say why) is:

How did the poem sound when it was read aloud?

What would be a good subject for the poet to try next?

What would be a good form for the next poem?

writing guides: POETRY